Special thanks to our adviser:
Susan Kesselring, M.A., Literacy Educator
Rosemount–Apple Valley–Eagan (Minnesota) School District

Some Porcupines Wrestle

and Other Freaky Facts About Animal Antics and Families

by Barbara Seuling
illustrated by Matthew Skeens

PICTURE WINDOW BOOKS
Minneapolis, Minnesota

Editors: Christianne Jones and Emmeline Elliott
Designer: Abbey Fitzgerald
Page Production: Melissa Kes
Art Director: Nathan Gassman
The illustrations in this book were created digitally.

Picture Window Books
5115 Excelsior Boulevard
Suite 232
Minneapolis, MN 55416
877-845-8392
www.picturewindowbooks.com

Text Copyright © 2008 by Barbara Seuling
Illustrations Copyright © 2008 by Picture Window Books

All rights reserved. No part of this book may be reproduced without written permission from the publisher. The publisher takes no responsibility for the use of any of the materials or methods described in this book, nor for the products thereof.

Printed in the United States of America.

 All books published by Picture Window Books are manufactured with paper containing at least 10 percent post-consumer waste.

Library of Congress Cataloging-in-Publication Data
Seuling, Barbara.
Some porcupines wrestle : and other freaky facts about animal antics and families / by Barbara Seuling ; illustrated by Matthew Skeens.
p. cm. — (Freaky facts)
Includes index.
ISBN 978-1-4048-4114-7 (library binding)
1. Animals—Miscellanea—Juvenile literature. I. Skeens, Matthew.
II. Title.
QL49.S43 2008
590—dc22   2007032919

Table of Contents

Chapter 1 — Good Times: Antics and Amusements...........4

Chapter 2 — You Were Meant for Me: Mating...........7

Chapter 3 — In the Nursery: Baby Care...........14

Chapter 4 — Camouflage and Other Clever Tricks: Survival Tactics...........22

Chapter 5 — You Scratch My Back, I'll Scratch Yours: Strange Relationships...........30

Chapter 6 — Once Upon a Time: Legends and Myths...........34

Glossary...........36
Index...........38
To Learn More...........40

Chapter 7

Good Times:
Antics and Amusements

Male porcupines sometimes wrestle for fun.

Deer play a game of tag. The one who is "it" taps the other with its hooves.

When a baby kangaroo jumps into its mother's pouch, it completes a full somersault inside the pouch. Then it twists around to face out.

North American gray wolf pups are encouraged to play when they are young. Adult wolves even dig out play areas near the den for the pups. The pups play tag with each other, scare each other by jumping out of hiding places, and play with feathers.

If you see an eastern spotted skunk do a handstand, stand back. It's usually a signal that the skunk is about to spray.

When playing, bears like to tumble down hills head over heels.

Adult squirrels are very playful. They turn somersaults, zip around in games of chase, roll around in leaves, climb to the ends of bouncy branches, and sway playfully in the breeze.

Badgers play leapfrog and turn somersaults on the grass.

The lyrebird mimics just about anything it hears. It can imitate 12 other birds and sounds, including a car engine, a car alarm, and a chainsaw.

Crows play pranks. One of their favorite tricks is sneaking up on a sleeping rabbit or cow and making a loud noise to wake it.

Penguins slide across the snow and ice on their stomachs.

Young otters play a sliding game, too. They take a few quick, short steps, and then push off for a long slide across ice, mudbanks, or snow slopes.

Sea otter mothers float on their backs in the water as they play with their babies, lifting them into the air and kissing them.

Fish have been known to be playful. Some fish have even squirted water at people.

You Were Meant for Me: Mating

Male bowerbirds construct fancy houses to lure a mate. The structures are decorated with brightly colored or glittering objects, such as bits of colored glass, beetle wings, bones, feathers, and berries.

The male magnificent frigatebird uses its bright red chin to attract a mate. When looking for a mate, he fills his chin with air and puffs it up like a balloon. This signals to a female that he has chosen a site for a nest.

A female red-necked phalarope bird courts a male, lays eggs, and then leaves. The male is left to do all of the work.

Chapter Two

After mating, the male African hornbill bird puts his mate in the hollow of a tree or cave. Only a small opening remains, through which he passes food to her. Inside, the female lays her eggs. She does not leave until her eggs hatch.

To show the female peacock that he is the best choice as a mate, the male peacock fans and rattles his tail feathers.

Before mating, elephants spend weeks getting to know each other. A couple will stand for hours and use their trunks in a playful tug-of-war.

You Were Meant for Me: Mating

Female seahorses lay their eggs directly into the male's pouch. He carries the eggs around until they hatch.

Off the coast of Dorset in Great Britain, spider crabs meet to breed every August. In some years, more than 50,000 spider crabs have gathered to mate.

One of the most incredible mating rituals happens between the largest creatures that exist—blue whales. They dive deep into the sea and jump out of the water, belly to belly. They mate in midair.

Male fiddler crabs have one claw that is much bigger than the other. They use the larger claw to attract females and warn other males to stay away from their part of the beach.

The swordtail fish of Mexico changes sex in the middle of its life. While it is female, it has babies. When it becomes a male, it fertilizes eggs.

Certain fish off the California coast come onto the beaches once each year during high tide. They ride the waves to shore by the thousands to lay their eggs in the sand.

Chapter Two

Right after he hatches, the male anglerfish grabs onto his sister with his teeth and hangs on until the skin of the female actually grows around him. He is now a part of her. As the female grows, the male remains a small addition growing out of her skin, becoming useful only when he is needed to fertilize her eggs.

The Surinam toad rolls eggs over the female's back and fertilizes them. The eggs settle into little pockets in her skin where they develop. When they hatch, tiny little toads seem to burst out of their mother's back.

You Were Meant for Me: Mating

In some species of whiptail lizard there are no males. The females give birth without mating. They only give birth to females, so the process continues. This is also true for many female insects.

Chameleons do not change color to match their surroundings. Their color changes according to their willingness to mate. It may also change according to their mood or temperature.

Most slugs and snails have both male and female organs. After mating, both genders can lay eggs.

Earthworms mate on damp nights. This keeps their bodies from drying out.

The horseshoe worm breeds using a process called budding. A small new worm attaches and grows on the body of an adult worm. Slowly, the new worm gets bigger and breaks away.

Glowworms aren't really worms at all. They are female beetles. The wingless female makes a glowing light to attract the male beetles, who fly to her and mate.

Chapter Two

The mayfly has only one day to live. During this day, the mayfly mates, molts twice, and lays eggs. It does not have a working mouth. It doesn't have time to eat during its lifetime.

The queen termite spends her life in a secure part of the nest preparing to lay eggs. Worker termites feed her, and she grows to be more than 100 times bigger than the other termites. She can lay as many as 1,000 eggs a day.

To signal their intention to mate and to calm the females, male jumping spiders perform mating dances.

You Were Meant for Me: Mating

A female praying mantis will eat anything she sees moving, including her mate. The male has to sneak up on her in order to mate. After the male and female mate, the male has a slim chance of escaping.

Male bumblebees attract females by leaving a scented chemical on leaves and twigs. A female bumblebee will find a scented spot and wait for her mate. After the bumblebees mate, the male dies.

Female moths give off a special scent when they are ready to mate. A male moth can smell a female from more than 2 miles (3.2 km) away.

In 1859, a clergyman in Australia released 24 rabbits into the world. In just six years, those 24 rabbits became 22 million rabbits.

Some animals have been crossed with each other successfully. A lion and a tiger, for example, produced a liger; a leopard and a jaguar have produced a jagulep; and a zebra and a donkey have produced a zedonk.

A skunk uses its spray as a perfume to attract mates.

Chapter 3

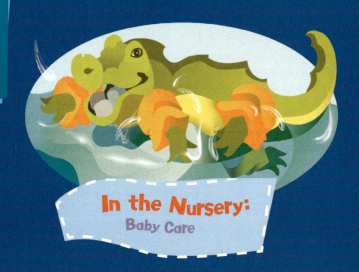

In the Nursery:
Baby Care

Baby crocodiles thrash around in the water doing the dog paddle to stay afloat. Only after they swallow some stones, which are used for digestion, do they gain the proper balance to swim smoothly.

When crocodile eggs hatch, the mother takes them in her mouth, marches down to the water, and swishes them around in her mouth to wash off all of the sand.

When an alligator's eggs are incubated below 86 F (30 C), all females are born. If the temperature is above 91 F (33 C), the offspring are male.

The male Darwin frog takes care of the tadpoles. Shortly after they are born, he swallows them. The young grow in his vocal sac. After three weeks, the tadpoles are tiny frogs and are ready to be on their own.

A blind salamander has two birth options. She can lay eggs or keep them inside and give birth to live young.

Hammerhead sharks do not take care of their babies. Sharks are born knowing how to swim and hunt.

A baby blue whale starts out at about 2.2 tons (2 metric tons). It gains an additional 198 pounds (89 kg) a day until it reaches its full growth, which is about 165 tons (149 metric tons).

Every day for the first eight months of life, baby blue whales drink more than 26 gallons (99 L) of milk from their mothers.

Chapter Three

Harp seal babies may not survive a warm winter in the Arctic. The adult females need to crawl out of the water onto the ice to have their babies. If all of the ice is melted, the pups will drown.

Although they spend most of their lives in the water, sea lions do not swim naturally. Mothers have to teach their babies the fine points of swimming.

After the female emperor penguin lays an egg, she leaves. The male rests the egg on top of his feet and keeps it warm with a fold of his belly skin. After two months, the female comes to take her turn, and the male leaves to eat.

Although the female cod lays about 5 million eggs a year, only a few of the fish will survive to become adults.

Hippos have their babies underwater. They also nurse their young underwater.

Scientifically speaking, the platypus is a mammal, yet it has a hard time producing milk.

In the Nursery: Baby Care

The mouth of a male mouthbreeder fish acts as a sort of garage for as many as 400 of his offspring. He holds them in his mouth to protect them from harm. If one tiny stranger gets in with the brood, the father spits it out without losing any of his own.

Moose mothers sometimes carry their babies on their backs to cross wide bodies of water.

Elephant mothers have used their tusks as forklifts to carry their babies across rivers.

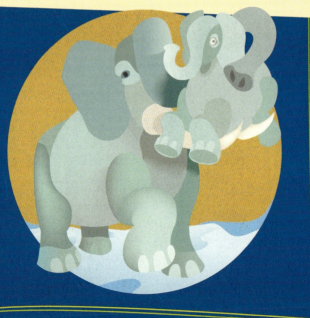

Chapter Three

Female kangaroos are almost always pregnant. As soon as one baby is fully out of the pouch, a new baby is born.

A kangaroo mother almost always is nursing babies of different ages. She has two different supplies of milk.

A baby kangaroo, or joey, uses its sense of smell to crawl through its mother's fur and find the warm pouch.

Baby giraffes drop several feet to the ground when they are born.

When the mother lion goes off to hunt, another female stays with the cubs. When the mother gets back, she shares her food.

When giving birth, the female porcupine is not injured by its baby's quills because the newborn is covered in a protective sac.

In the Nursery: Baby Care

The nine-banded armadillo almost always has four babies at a time, all the same sex, and identical in every way.

The opossum gives birth to about 15 babies at a time, each the size of a honeybee.

Every hamster in the world is a descendant of one female hamster.

Chapter Three

To protect her new babies, a female wolf spider carries her young on her back. The young hang on to special knob-shaped hairs so they don't fall off.

Young cicadas stay underground for protection. The bugs suck juices from roots to grow. Some stay underground for 17 years before coming out as adults.

A greylag gosling will follow the first object it sees moving after it hatches. The gosling then adopts that object as its mother. It could be a dog, a ball, or even a car!

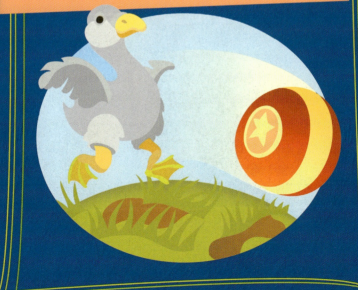

In the Nursery: Baby Care

Most baby birds are born with a single tooth, which helps them peck their way out of their shells. After the big breakout, the tooth disappears.

The cuckoo doesn't build its own nest. Instead, it leaves its egg in another bird's nest. When the egg hatches, the newly-hatched cuckoo bird throws out the other eggs and claims the nest.

Megapodes, big thick-legged birds, lay their eggs on a pile of rotting vegetation. The heat from the pile incubates and hatches the eggs. With their responsibilities behind them, the parent birds take off, never returning. Fortunately, the young are born ready to take care of themselves. A minute after hatching, a young bird can fly.

When baby ostriches are frightened, they squat and flatten themselves out as much as possible so they barely cast a shadow.

Parent birds remove all traces of eggshell from their nests after their young are hatched so the light color of the shell lining doesn't attract predators.

Chapter 4

Camouflage and Other Clever Tricks: Survival Tactics

Spiders weave signs of warning into their webs to keep birds and large insects from flying into and damaging their webs.

Each of a spider's eight legs can bend in six places. That means a spider has 48 knees. If a spider loses a leg, it will grow a new one.

To protect themselves from predators, some walking sticks will sway so they look like a stick blowing in the breeze.

Leaf insects disguise their eggs as well as themselves. The bugs drop their eggs on the ground. There, the eggs look like seeds.

The queen bee is the only honeybee in the hive that can sting more than once. After a female worker honeybee stings her victim, she loses her stinger and dies. Male bees do not have stingers.

Arctic bumblebees shiver to generate heat. Their thick hair traps the heat they are producing from shivering and keeps them warm.

When a ladybug feels threatened, it pulls its six legs completely inside of its body and pretends to be dead.

When threatened, the bombardier beetle blasts its victim with a small explosion of stinging chemicals.

Chapter Four

The assassin bug is a master of disguise. It hides behind the carcasses of its dead enemies to get closer to live termites. When a termite comes to help cart away the dead body, the assassin bug jumps out and attacks it.

The spider crab is a smart dresser. It cuts off pieces of live sponges and wears them on its back. The sponge pieces grow around the spider crab to fit. Since sponges taste awful, most animals leave them alone. In its smart sponge suit, the spider crab is protected.

Camouflage and Other Clever Tricks: Survival Tactics

When a spiny sea cucumber is threatened, it squirts its internal organs at the predator. While the predator is distracted, the spiny sea cucumber escapes. It grows new organs quickly.

The Australian sea dragon, a type of sea horse, has leafy-looking extensions growing out of its body. The extensions look just like the vines and leaves of seaweed. Its only defense is to hide itself from enemies with these parts of its own body.

According to some experts, dolphins send bubbles to the surface to relay messages to other dolphins. They also make clicking sounds to communicate with other dolphins, but no one has worked out exactly what they mean.

If attacked, an octopus squirts dark ink at the predator. The ink distracts the predator, and the octopus can escape to safety.

The electric eel can send off an electric charge strong enough to electrocute a person. Some eels are totally blind from eye damage caused by the electrical charges given off by their fellow eels.

Chapter Four

The golden poison-dart frog is the most deadly of all the poison-dart frogs. The skin of just one frog contains enough poison to kill more than 1,000 people.

The horned toad shoots a stream of blood from each of its eyes when it is upset.

Many lizards, when grabbed by the tail, let their tails snap off and make a fast getaway. A new tail grows later, but without a bone structure to support it.

A porcupine has about 30,000 sharp quills, each one equipped with tiny barbs. Needless to say, the porcupine doesn't have many enemies.

The only place porcupines don't have sharp quills is on their soft bellies, so they work hard to stay upright and protected.

Baby deer spend a lot of time curled up near plants on the forest floor. The white spots on their coats blend in with the patches of sunlight shining through the leaves. The spots are the perfect camouflage from predators.

Camouflage and Other Clever Tricks: Survival Tactics

The sound of wolves howling is often the howl of a single wolf. The sound is made up of many sounds. This gives the impression that there are more animals than there actually are.

The camel spreads out its toes when it walks on sand. This tactic makes the camel's feet extra wide, which keeps the camel from sinking into the sand.

In certain types of light, the spray of a skunk glows.

Chapter Four

The fennec fox has fur on the bottom of its feet. The fur helps protect it from the hot desert sand.

Cats have a thick pad under each toe. Because cats walk on their toes, the pads help them to walk very quietly and go undetected around predators.

The snowshoe hare turns from brown to white in the winter, making it practically invisible in the snow.

A thick layer of blubber helps keep the polar bear warm while swimming in cold water.

The skin underneath a polar bear's fur is black. The dark color helps trap heat from the sun to keep the big animal warm in the cold Arctic.

The musk ox has broad hooves that spread out flat. These flat feet help keep the ox from sinking into the deep snow.

A snow leopard has extra fur on the bottom of its paws for protection against snow and ice.

Camouflage and Other Clever Tricks: Survival Tactics

Thick fat and layers of thick feathers keep the emperor penguin warm in freezing weather.

Snowy owls protect themselves from the cold with lots of extra feathers. Their feathers cover most of their beak and their feet.

The ptarmigan bird turns white in the winter to blend in with its snowy surroundings.

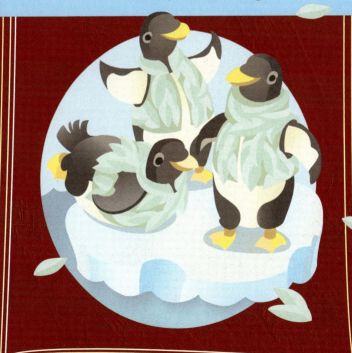

Chapter 5

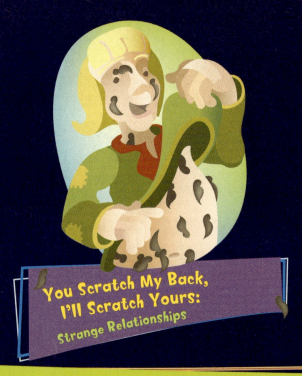

You Scratch My Back, I'll Scratch Yours: Strange Relationships

Leeches were used by European physicians in the Middle Ages to cure all kinds of sickness. For a fever, a band of leeches was placed around the head. For indigestion, 20 or 30 were placed on the stomach.

In the 18th and 19th centuries, leeches became even more popular. There was such a huge American demand for them that about 30 million were shipped from Germany to the United States every year. In more modern applications, leeches have been used by boxers to drain black eyes and on patients after plastic surgery.

Earthworms are a farmer's delight. In one year, the earthworms in 1 acre (0.4 hectare) of soil can turn over about 18 tons (16 metric tons) of soil.

Ladybugs help farmers and gardeners by eating aphids, which are little insects that harm plants and crops.

The anemone and the clownfish help each other. The anemone offers protection to the clownfish. In return, the clownfish keeps the anemone clean by eating its leftovers.

Pond snails are often used to keep aquariums clean. As the snail moves, it scrapes off the green gunk that builds up on the glass of fish tanks.

In a pinch, snowy tree crickets can be used instead of thermometers. Count the number of chirps a cricket makes in 15 seconds, add 40, and the result is the Fahrenheit temperature, within about two degrees.

Snakes have helped scientists in the study of human diseases and cures.

Chapter Five

A rare kind of silk comes from the pinna marina, or giant silk-bearded clam, found in the Mediterranean Sea. Its long strands of milky secretions were once spun into fine cloth and traded in Spain, Italy, and North Africa.

Sea lions and dolphins have been trained by the U.S. Navy to work with submarine rockets and mines for undersea war operations.

New York City has a horses' rights bill. It bans horses from being forced to work in temperatures of 90 F (32 C) or more. It also demands that they have 15 minutes of rest for every two hours of work.

International treaties have been made over the use of bat and bird droppings, which are the richest fertilizer on Earth. The largest deposits are on islands off the coast of Peru.

Poodles were first clipped to make it easier for them to swim. They were brought along by hunters to retrieve birds that were shot down.

You Scratch My Back, I'll Scratch Yours: Strange Relationships

For centuries, the Japanese cormorant has been used to help catch fish. The bird is trained to swoop down, catch a fish, and carry it back to the fishing boat.

A major missile maker once switched from messengers on motorcycles to carrier pigeons to deliver material to its research facility 64 miles (102 km) away. The pigeons were twice as fast and cost a lot less.

Two hand puppets resembling a California condor's parents were used to hand feed a condor chick at the San Diego Zoo. The zoo, dedicated to helping the endangered birds, has a large breeding facility known as the Condorminium.

Chapter 6

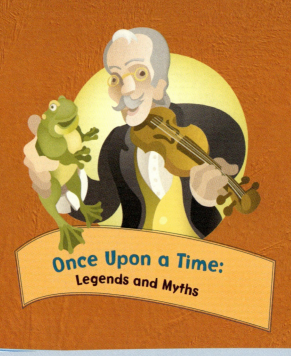

Once Upon a Time:
Legends and Myths

Violinists once handled toads before a concert. They believed the secretions of the animal would keep their hands from sweating.

In the Middle Ages, stories spread in many European countries about werewolves who would attack humans. The Danes, for example, believed that if a man's eyebrows met, he would become a werewolf. French and German tradition held that a child born with teeth would grow up to be a warewolf.

The ancient Egyptians worshipped cats. A person could be executed for killing one.

The stork is considered good luck to many Europeans. Some people even put platforms on their roofs to encourage the birds to nest there.

In medieval Italy, people believed that if a person was bitten by a wolf spider, frantic dancing would rid the victim's body of the spider's poison.

One of the two teeth of the male narwhal whale sticks out from its jaw in a long spiral. In the Middle Ages, travelers brought many of these teeth home, claiming that they were unicorns' horns with magical powers.

For centuries, a powdered rhinoceros horn has been used in some cultures in the belief that it has medical uses. As a result, one kind of rhinoceros is nearly extinct.

In ancient Greece, killing a dolphin was considered as bad as killing a person.

Manatees were responsible for tales of mermaid sightings. These large marine mammals, seen at a distance bobbing upright in the water while holding their babies between their flippers, must have looked human to sailors who had been at sea for a very long time.

Glossary

antic—a playful or funny act or action

breed—to mate and produce young

brood—a group of young that were born at the same time

camouflage—a pattern or color on an animal's skin that makes it blend in with the things around it

carcasses—bodies of dead animals

descendant—a person or animal who comes from a particular group of ancestors

digestion—the process a body uses to turn food into energy

diseases—sicknesses

disguise—to hide by looking like something else

extensions—additions

fertilize—to make fertile

incubate—to sit on eggs and keep them warm so they hatch

larvae—the newly hatched form of some insects; larvae have a soft body and look like a worm

mammal—a warm-blooded animal that feeds its babies milk

mate—the male or female of a pair of animals

mates—joins together to produce young

mimic—to copy

molts—sheds fur, feathers, or an outer layer of skin

nursing—how a mother feeds her babies milk

offspring—the young of a person, animal, or plant

predators—animals that hunt and eat other animals

secretions—substances released by an animal

somersault—to roll by turning the heels over the head

tactics—methods planned to achieve a goal

thrash—to make wild movements

Index

African hornbills, 8
alligators, 15
anemones, 31
anglerfish, 10
armadillos, 19
assassin bugs, 24
Australian sea dragons, 25

badgers, 5
bat droppings, 32
bears, 5, 28
beetles, 11, 23
bird droppings, 32
blue whales, 9, 15
bombardier beetles, 23
bowerbirds, 7
budding, 11
bumblebees, 13, 23

California condors, 33
camels, 27
carrier pigeons, 33
cats, 28, 34
chameleons, 11
cicadas, 20
clownfish, 31
cod, 16
Condominium, 33
crocodiles, 14
crows, 5
cuckoo, 21

Darwin frogs, 15
deer, 4, 26
dolphins, 25, 32, 35
donkeys, 13
droppings, 32

earthworms, 11, 31
eggs, 7, 8, 9, 10, 11, 12, 14, 15, 16, 21, 23
electric eels, 25
elephants, 8, 17
emperor penguins, 16, 29

fennec foxes, 28
fertilization, 9, 10, 12
fiddler crabs, 9
frogs, 15, 26

giant silk-bearded clams, 32
giraffes, 18
glowworms, 11
gray wolves, 5
greylag goslings, 20

hammerhead sharks, 15
hamsters, 19
harp seals, 16
hippos, 16
honeybees, 23
horned toads, 26
horses, 32
horseshoe worms, 11

jaguars, 13
jaguleps, 13
Japanese cormorants, 33
jumping spiders, 12

kangaroos, 4, 18

ladybugs, 23, 31
leaf insects, 23
leeches, 30
leopards, 13, 28
ligers, 13
lions, 13, 18
lyrebirds, 5

magnificent frigatebirds, 7
manatees, 35
mating, 7, 8, 9, 10, 11, 12, 13
mayflies, 12
megapodes, 21
moose, 17
moths, 13
mouthbreeder fish, 17
musk oxen, 28

narwhals, 35
nursing, 15, 16, 18

octopuses, 25
opossums, 19
ostriches, 21
otters, 6

peacocks, 8
penguins, 6, 16, 29
phalarope birds, 7
pinna marinas, 32
platypuses, 16
poison-dart frogs, 26
polar bears, 28
poodles, 32
porcupines, 4, 18, 26
praying mantises, 13
ptarmigan birds, 29

rabbits, 13
rhinoceroses, 35

salamanders, 15
San Diego Zoo, 33
sea horses, 9, 25
sea lions, 16, 32
sharks, 15
skunks, 5, 13, 27
slugs, 11
snails, 11, 31

snakes, 31
snow leopards, 28
snowshoe hares, 28
snowy owls, 29
snowy tree crickets, 31
spider crabs, 9, 24
spiders, 12, 20, 22, 35
spiny sea cucumbers, 25
sponges, 24
squirrels, 5
storks, 35
Surinam toads, 10
swordtail fish, 9

tadpoles, 15
teeth, 10, 21, 34, 35
termites, 12, 24
tigers, 13
toads, 10, 26, 34

walking sticks, 23
werewolves, 34
whales, 9, 15, 35
whiptail lizards, 11
wolf spiders, 20, 35
wolves, 5, 27

zebras, 13
zedonks, 13

To Learn More

More Books to Read

De Ford, Deborah. *I Wonder Why Skunks Are So Smelly: And Other Neat Facts About Mammals*. Racine, Wis.: Western Pub. Co., 1992.

Mattern, Joanne, and Ryan Herndon. *Guinness World Records. Astonishing Animals*. New York: Scholastic, 2005.

Petty, Kate. *Animal Camouflage and Defense*. Philadelphia: Chelsea House Publishers, 2005.

On the Web

FactHound offers a safe, fun way to find Web sites related to topics in this book. All of the sites on FactHound have been researched by our staff.

1. Visit *www.facthound.com*
2. Type in this special code: 1404841148
3. Click on the FETCH IT button.

Your trusty FactHound will fetch the best sites for you.

Look for all of the books in the Freaky Facts series:

Ancient Coins Were Shaped Like Hams: and Other Freaky Facts About Coins, Bills, and Counterfeiting

Cows Sweat Through Their Noses and Other Freaky Facts About Animal Habits, Characteristics, and Homes

Earth Is Like a Giant Magnet and Other Freaky Facts About Planets, Oceans, and Volcanoes

One President was Born on Independence Day and Other Freaky Facts About the 26th Through 43rd Presidents

Some Porcupines Wrestle and Other Freaky Facts About Animal Antics and Families

Three Presidents Died on the Fourth of July and Other Freaky Facts About the First 25 Presidents

Your Skin Weighs More Than Your Brain and Other Freaky Facts About Your Skin, Skeleton, and Other Body Parts